MY TEACHER CAN TEACH... ANYONE!

by W. Nikola-Lisa

illustrations by Felipe Galindo

SCHOOL PUBLISHERS

Visit The Learning Site!
www.harcourtschool.com

This edition is published by special arrangement with Lee & Low Books Inc.,
New York.

Grateful acknowledgment is made to Lee & Low Books Inc., New York, for
permission to reprint *My Teacher Can Teach...Anyone!* by W. Nikola-Lisa,
illustrated by Felipe Galindo. Text copyright © 2004 by W. Nikola-Lisa;
illustrations copyright © 2004 by Felipe Galindo.

Printed in China

ISBN 10 0-15-352468-5
ISBN 13 978-0-15-352468-4

2 3 4 5 6 7 8 9 10   985   15 14 13 12 11 10 09 08 07

To the teacher in you, Larissa —W.N.-L.

For Andrea with love —F.G.

My teacher is so good,

she can teach...*anyone!*

She could teach an Astronaut
how to float in space.

She could teach a Ballet dancer
how to land with grace.

She could teach a Carpenter
how to nail a roof.

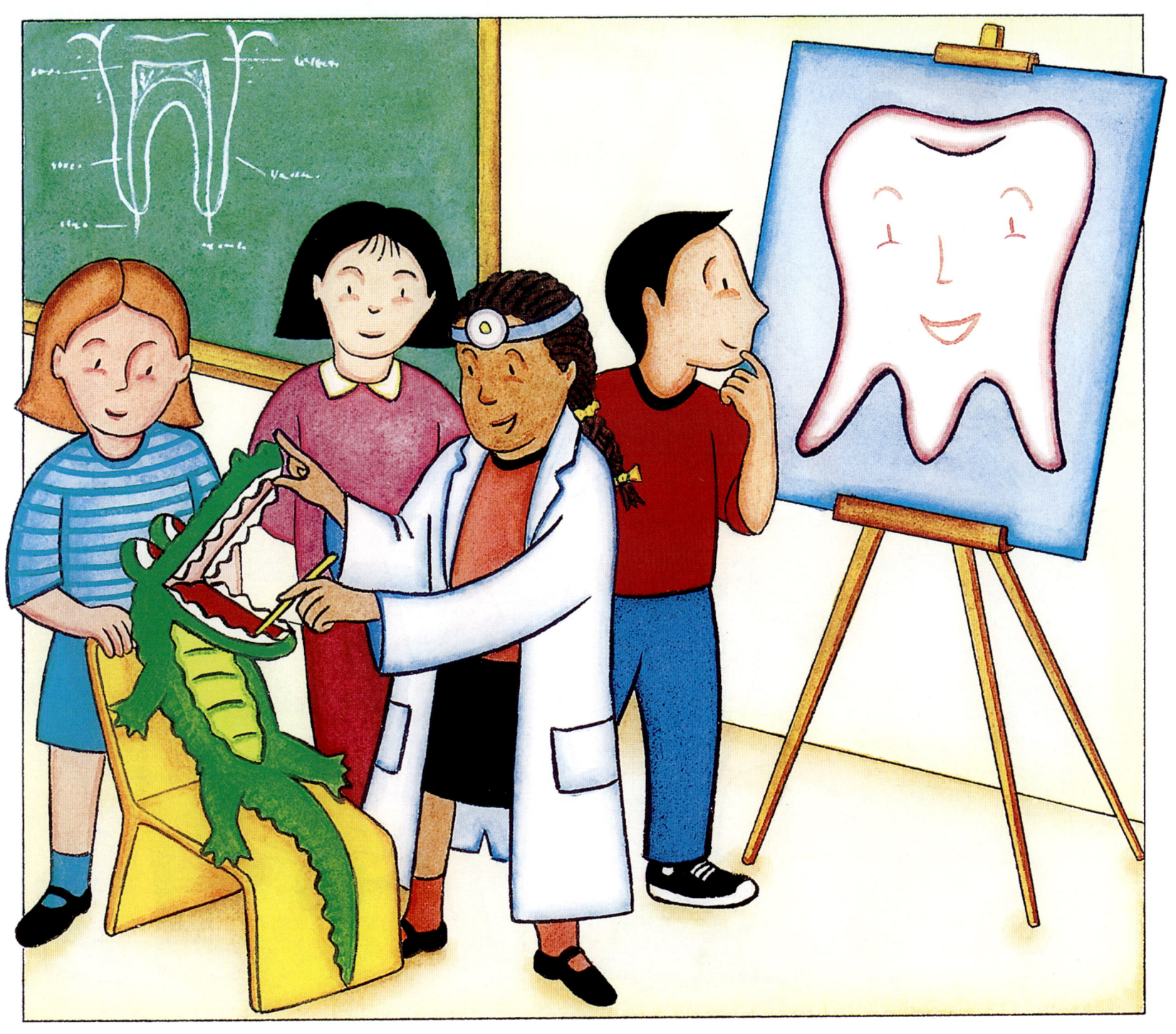

She could teach a Dentist
how to fill a tooth.

She could teach an Engineer
how to dig a hole.

She could teach a Firefighter
how to slide the pole.

She could teach the Governor
how to host a lunch.

She could teach a Heavyweight
how to throw a punch.

She could teach an Illustrator
how to draw a top.

She could teach a Janitor
how to wring a mop.

She could teach a Kayaker
how to pull a stroke.

She could teach a Logger
how to fell an oak.

She could teach a Mechanic
how to change a hose.

She could teach a Novelist
how to write in prose.

She could teach an Opera singer
how to hold a note.

She could teach the President
how to cast a vote.

She could teach a Quarterback
how to throw a ball.

She could teach a Rodeo clown
how to take a fall.

She could teach a Sailor
how to cast a jig.

She could teach a Trucker
how to drive a rig.

She could teach an Umpire
how to call an out.

She could teach a Veterinarian
how to hold a snout.

She could teach a Woodworker
how to build a trap.

She could teach a Xylophonist
how to play with snap.

She could teach a Yodeler
how to sing a mile.

She could teach a Zillionaire
how to live in style.